Just Say Yes to Life

Embracing Individuation
to Embrace Life

Just Say Yes to Life

Embracing Individuation
to Embrace Life

Patricia Caldwell-Lee

BOOKS

Winchester, UK
Washington, USA

First published by O-Books, 2012
O-Books is an imprint of John Hunt Publishing Ltd., Laurel House, Station Approach,
Alresford, Hants, SO24 9JH, UK
office1@o-books.net
www.o-books.com

For distributor details and how to order please visit the 'Ordering' section on our website.

Text copyright: Patricia Caldwell-Lee 2010

ISBN: 978 1 84694 406 2

A CIP catalogue record for this book is available from the British Library.

Design: Lee Nash

Printed in the UK by CPI Antony Rowe
Printed in the USA by Offset Paperback Mfrs, Inc

We operate a distinctive and ethical publishing philosophy in all
areas of our business, from our global network of authors to
production and worldwide distribution.

CONTENTS

CONTENTS

I dedicate this book to my darling husband, Alan Lee.

Acknowledgements

With immense gratitude to the following: to the wonderful friends from the former Qdos committee: Pam Harris; Emma Isaac; Monika Key; and Julie Lawford who all gave me the impetus to write the book and give talks on the subject; to Satara Lester and Jill Mills, both psychologists, for their expert advice and support; to Jacqui Lofthouse, novelist, who gave such fantastic help and guided me through the publishing world; and to the many friends who read the proposal.

Introduction

'Just Say Yes to Life' demystifies the Jungian term 'individu-ation' and takes us on a compelling and fascinating journey on how to individuate fully: to become what or who you are destined to be.

Carl Jung, the renowned Swiss Psychologist, described individuation as an individual's journey to psychological wholeness. This book takes Jung's fascinating concept, explores it fully and brings it right up to date with a modern twist.

Essentially, individuation is an inner drive pushing or nudging us to become what or who we are destined to be. It gives us a powerful message that we need to develop and differentiate to fulfil our destiny. It is a significant adult developmental process which occurs throughout adult life and as we allow ourselves to continually individuate, we attract change and growth.

The book clarifies the many ways in which the process of individuation makes its presence known in our lives. For example, why do so many of us begin to question our lives when 'everything appears to be just right?' This process is charac-terised by an apparent 'rightness' on the surface accompanied by an inner lack of fulfilment. It is this realisation, that an inner lack of fulfilment, is actually our need to continue to individuate, to go out into the unknown and continue to evolve.

Illustrated by many interesting examples of those in the public eye who are individuating successfully, this book is also supplemented by visuals and questionnaires to help each reader discover where they are on the path of their own individuation. It fully explains the process and points out the significant indicators that raise our awareness of individuation, for example synchronistic occurrences and the relevance of the seven year cycle. In addition the book explores what happens if we suppress the process of individuation, as the majority of us do. Most importantly it outlines the steps needed to individuate fully.

Individuation gives us an understanding that our lives do not simply unfold in accordance with an inner blueprint, but have a divine or cosmic significance. If we are to fulfil our human potential, it is essential that we *individuate*.

The Wake Up Call - My Story

In 2001, I made the decision to quit at the top of a very lucrative and successful career in Hotel Management.

I had spent twelve wonderful, fun and hard working years in the hotel industry and many people both friends and colleagues thought I was crazy to give up such a prestigious position. Even as I started thinking about making a change I had no idea what else I might like to do. I distinctly remembered though, questioning what life was all about. Why, had I an inner lack of fulfilment, when outwardly everything appeared just right? Cosmologists call this – *when everything is just right* – the 'Goldilocks effect'.

I was not able to identify what this was, yet I felt I needed to develop more of myself. I knew that there had to be something more even though I had achieved many of my material goals, another part of me was unfulfilled. Interestingly, the global Personnel Director of the Hotel Group, who was exceptionally well respected and had built up a wonderful career, was visiting the hotel I was working at. She mentioned to me that she was leaving to become a teacher of blind children. I remembered being shocked by her decision. It was such a sudden career change, it seemed she was giving up so much, yet I thought 'why not?' It was an event that, unbeknown to me then, would help me with my decision to leave the hotel industry in the future.

Let Synchronicity provide the connections

Shortly after this incident, as synchronicity would have it, I was invited to attend a lecture on Directions for Life. There were four women speakers and one of them was a professional coach and author. I remember thinking, this is what I want to do. I want to do motivational talks, be an executive coach, an author and on stage. I wanted to move forward to develop and grow though I still did not know how I was going to do this. I began investigating coaching academies of which there were very few at that time but once again providence provided the link. Because I had attended the lecture my name was on a mailing list which a new coaching academy had bought. As I was pondering what to do next, I received their information on coaching courses which proved to be just what I needed. The timing could not have been more perfect.

Keeping the Focus on What You Want
Eventually I found a coaching academy and was able to continue my work and study part time. After qualifying I knew it was time to leave the hotel industry, though I still felt incredibly uncomfortable with this idea. It was not an easy decision, in fact it was a difficult period and I was very apprehensive. I also asked the questions – where would I get clients?

Then incredibly, I received a call from my ex university, the University of Ulster, inviting me to give a talk at the Alumni Society on my change of direction. Although I was very apprehensive about doing the talk as I was only recently qualified I knew I had to *Just Say Yes* to this opportunity. It was a significant indicator from the Universe. Not only was the talk well received but several people signed up to coaching straight away. Additionally more clients followed and then the University did an editorial about my new direction in life in their Alumni magazine.

Remarkably, the clients I began coaching all came to me with the same issue I encountered two years previously – an inner lack of fulfilment accompanied by an apparent 'rightness' on the surface, in an otherwise successful life. I recalled being aware that this was much more than a significant synchronistic event and decided to research this phenomena. I read a book by Carol Adrienne, author of 'Find your Purpose , Change your Life' and came across the word *'individuation'*.

I had not heard of it before and when the definition was clarified to me, I immediately had an 'Aha' moment. I had a sense of liberation. This led me to coach on the process of individuation and to bring this subject into my talks. Not only did the invitation to speak set in motion my next career, but it became an example of the power of individuation.

The subject of becoming one's authentic self – the Jungian psychological maturation process - resonated with me and I realised that my inner lack of fulfilment was my need to continue to individuate, to go out into the unknown and continue to evolve. Intriguingly or possibly synchronistic, shortly after this came about, Carol Adrienne the author of the book where I first came across the word individuation, interviewed me for her American website magazine on my journey so far. Life had come full circle.

Chapter 1

What is individuation?

The term 'individuation' was first coined by Carl Jung. He described it as an individual's journey to psychological wholeness or 'becoming what or who you are destined to become'. Jung saw the whole life cycle as a continuing process of growth and change regulated by the Self. 'Individuation is an expression of that biological process – simple or complicated as the case may be- by which every living thing becomes what it is destined to become from the very beginning'.

Essentially, individuation is an inner drive, deep within the recesses of our soul, giving us a powerful message that we need to develop and differentiate. It is a significant adult developmental process which occurs throughout adult life and as we allow ourselves to continually individuate we attract change and growth. Jung states that 'Individuation', therefore is a process of differentiation, having for its goal the development of the individual personality'.

If we are to fulfil our human potential, we must individuate. Jung asserted that the deepest urge or instinct within every living creature is to fulfil itself and he called this *life long process* that aims at *fulfilment*, 'Individuation'.

Ultimately, individuation is the merging of the ego (the conscious mind) and the self (the unconscious mind) to work in unison. Both are mutually independent and one cannot survive without the other. To achieve this mergence, the ego and self initially separate and go through various stages of development, from a biological and social period to the cultural and spiritual (ego and the self diagram attached).In the early part of adulthood, up to the age of approximately 28-35 we have ego independence, a relative lack of self, we are ego driven. It is essentially a 'biological and social period ', where we focus on 'Personal Identity ' i.e. who we are, not, what we are to become.

At this stage we compare ourselves to our peers and relate most effectively in groups. Although we are growing up and individuating, we are going through similar changes and during this phase in most cases we have no desire to stand out from the crowd. We are selfish, materialistic and driven in our work, moving through adulthood encompassing the normal things i.e. relationships, gap years, marriage, children, and settling into a career. It is interesting to note and to emphasise that in astrology the age of 29yrs is exceptionally significant. This is the time of the 'Saturn return' the first time the planet Saturn has returned to our chart since birth. Saturn is the planet of responsibility and seeks to give us an innate sense of discipline. The timing from the universe in conjunction with this stage of individuation could not be more perfect.

When we are individuating during this time, we feel very little discomfort as our peers are behaving in a similar way. It feels natural. However, although this biological and social period is vitally important, it does lead to an inevitable imbalance in our lifestyle. The psyche does though seek to redress this in later life. However during this first development stage it allows us to become independent from the parent

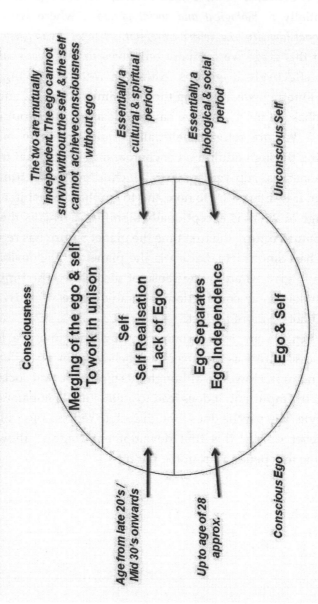

INDIVIDUATION

A process of differentiation – the goal of individuation is the development of the individual personality.

Consciousness

The two are mutually independent. The ego cannot survive without the self & the self cannot achieve consciousness without ego

Essentially a cultural & spiritual period

Essentially a biological & social period

Unconscious Self

Merging of the ego & self
To work In unison

Self
Self Realisation
Lack of Ego

Ego Separates
Ego Independence

Ego & Self

Age from late 20's / Mid 30's onwards

Up to age of 28 approx.

Conscious Ego

The EGO & The SELF: THE INDIVIDUAL

and to lay strong foundations for the future. According to Jung, during this period of adulthood the ego struggles to be free from the mother and assert its independence, developing a sense of independence from self while remaining intimately connected to it. When we participate fully here, we are able to adapt more easily to the often more challenging cultural and spiritual period which follows.

Moving through to this next stage during our late thirties, early to late forties, individuation does become more acceptable as we begin to understand it more fully. It still can though be a very disruptive influence, giving rise to an uncertain time. However, as individuation is an adult psychological process, an inner drive from our soul, we are gently nudged, initially, by the universe to move forward. Of course, we can ignore this push, but by doing so only makes us more uncomfortable.

This period, where we go through profound change is deemed *cultural and spiritual* and our aim is for self-realisation and lack of ego. We want to go beyond the ego and discover the self. It is when we become aware of our own mortality, the passing of time. We focus on our legacy, our achievements and the meaning of life. A sense of urgency takes over.

It is only really in mid-life during this cultural and spiritual period when we seek to discover the meaning of life that the real process of individuation and growing up takes place. In fact, the patients who interested Jung the most, were those seeking a meaning to their lives, who were often materially successful but felt empty and unfulfilled. They were in the cultural and spiritual phase of self-realisation and letting go of the ego. Moving from the biological & social period through to cultural and spiritual is often difficult, and uncomfortable with many preferring to stay in the comfort of the ego building activities of first adulthood. This is when the majority of people suppress individuation.

Most importantly, Individuation has to be worked for. It is not an easy process – it requires courage and dedication. Growth and change does not just happen of its own accord; Jung warns us that making our own 'journey through the unconscious'- to enlighten our egos – is hard work, a great labour in which the ego must accept full responsibility for all that occurs.

Here, in this period we also become more separated from our peers, we are more alone and no longer belong in a set group. This is when we notice ourselves changing, individuating more acutely and it is the reason why we start to question our lives.

When we differentiate, this becomes more noticeable to others (and many would prefer us not to change). This can increase our own awareness of our aloneness and increase our anxiety of what or who we are becoming.

The' persecution of those who are different' prevents many of us fromindividuating fully. The story of Frankenstein, published in 1818, reveals this. It was written by Mary Shelly after having a nightmare during a stormy night whilst staying with her husband at Lord Byron's Swiss villa beside Lake Geneva. Although in her story Frankenstein was deemed a dangerous monster by the public, Mary Shelley wanted to draw attention to the fact that he was persecuted only for being different, not dangerous.

However, being different makes all of us uncomfortable. It highlights our own inadequacies, our own sameness. Although we initially might embrace another's difference, or quirkiness, it soon becomes unappealing as we compare ourselves unfavourably. We then look for ways to disassociate ourselves and to question being different. Hence, Frankenstein became betrayed as a monster, giving a credible reason to those who felt uncomfortable with his difference, to persecute him. Another wonderful example of this, is the film of Edward Scissorhands, directed by Tim Burton. A wonderful modern day fairytale -the monster with a heart, he is the freak in suburban neighbourhood and becomes the local hero. His creator died just before he was given hands so he had scissor hands and lived on his own on the top of the mountain without human contact. He was befriended by one of the neighbours who sought to rehabilitate him and in doing so he became a hero and loved by the community until his differences became a threat and he was shunned. Once his differences were no longer enchanting and ' different' he, once again like Frankenstein, becomes persecuted. It dramatises the isolation one can experience by being different.

It is at this stage when many of us decide to take the easier option of staying in the biological and social ego driven period that we automatically suppress our individuation. Sadly many of us do and of course that is why we come across so many at this age who are unable to let go and are still living, regrettably unhappily, very much in this ego first phase of life.

However, we need to be strong to relinquish the ego and when we do, we open ourselves to greater wonder and the rewards are truly great. We liberate ourselves and start becoming who we are destined to be. A very clear example of someone relinquishing his ego and moving effortlessly to the cultural and spiritual stage, is Bill Gates. At the age of 42, he made a decision in conjunction with his wife, to create the Melinda Gates fund, a charity working with third world issues and worth millions of pounds. At the same time, he declared that he would step down within seven years, from the chairmanship of Microsoft, the company he set up at university with his childhood friend. This he did at the age of 49 years.

Another very clear example of moving through to this stage is that of Oprah Winfrey, the talk show host. Named as the world's most powerful celebrity and one of the most generous, she has realised one of her dreams. She has built a futuristic Academy, The Oprah Winfrey Leadership Academy for Girls. It is for the under-privileged and is based in South Africa. From early life, growing up with nothing, education has always been vitally important to her; it is her cause and this is part of her legacy.

11

Many of us now recognise that embracing individuation is an ultimately religious or spiritual undertaking. It is the conscious response to an innate and powerful drive toward ultimate meaning and wholeness. It places a huge responsibility on us, but a life without meaning i.e. individuating is a life not living authentically. Individuation is to be celebrated and embraced. It gives us an understanding that our lives do not simply unfold in accordance with an inner blueprint, but have a divine or cosmic significance.

As we individuate, we realise that we as human beings have a great need for purpose and meaning and the recognition of something greater than ourselves. Then individuation becomes a way of life and gives meaning to life. If we are to fulfil our human potential, it is essential that we individuate.

Chapter Two

How does individuation make its presence known in life?

This chapter describes the three stages of how individuation makes its presence known and how we can recognise it. It explains the events that can occur i.e. 'significant indicators' which give us our wake up calls to move along the path of individuation.

Stage One – 'The goldilocks effect' – *when everything is just right*

The first stage of how individuation makes its presence known is always characterised by an inner lack of fulfilment accompanied by an apparent 'rightness' on the surface, when 'everything appears to be just right'. When there is an inner lack of fulfilment, it is a significant indicator that we need to continue to individuate. We need to listen to the whispers of our soul. When we begin to listen the universe starts to gently nudge us to move us to the next stage of our lives. The first stage comes quietly, always in a whisper. It is not noticed or recognised by others, only by ourselves as it is still an inner feeling. This stage can last a number of years and it is easy to ignore as on the surface, our lives are perfect. During this stage we are usually in relationships we love, a career we enjoy, where we have achieved what we needed to achieve, and where others see our positions as ideal. This though is the perfect time to leave. But it takes great courage to leave at this time as others are unaware of your inner restlessness.

When James Truman the editorial director of Conde Nast told his employer, the chairman Samuel 'Si' Newhouse Jr, that he was leaving his powerful and prestigious post, the reaction was one of shock and surprise. Truman was at the time only 46yrs old and had been in the position from the age of 35yrs, with a reputed £2million salary and editorial authority over every US glossy magazine the company published. Yet, he found himself restless and becoming bored. His screensaver quoted the mythologist and adventurer Joseph Campbell 'We must be willing to get rid of the life we've planned so as to have the life that is waiting for us'. He said ' I grew bored. I felt I had achieved what I could in the job and didn't see it changing much going into the future, so I decided to step out of the picture'. He made a courageous decision and left at the top. The perfect time to leave– at the top or when you feel you have reached your nadir - and it is unexpected. Truman left at the first stage – when he heard the whispers, the nudges from the soul.

Do you have an inner lack of fulfilment? Remember it is *always* the first significant indicator of your inner self, your intuition, your heart, your soul, telling you it is time to individuate.

Stage Two – The whispers become louder, the 'soul' awakens
The second stage of individuation is more pronounced – the whispers are much louder, we begin to ask ourselves questions such as, what is the meaning of our lives, what is my purpose? We start to feel more uncomfortable, even emotional and become very aware of our own mortality. We begin to sense another kind of calling. Our soul starts to awaken and nudge us more deeply, to remind us of our purpose the reason for our being and our destiny. We start to notice more coincidences, and synchronistic events in our lives. Our behaviour changes outwardly and becomes noticed by others – we become more removed from our peers and less materialistic. Our work is less enjoyable, our relationships not as perfect. Life is not as easy.

Many celebrities mention a time just before they became known when things changed for them. For example, before Elton

John became famous, when he was still Reginald Dwight and struggling in the Dick James studios, he was in a group and toured the UK club circuit. After a while he started to become edgy, uncomfortable, dissatisfied and had an inner feeling of unfulfilment. These feelings continued, the group stopped making money, work was infrequent and he realised he was not doing something he loved. He was at stage two moving rapidly towards stage three. He knew his passion was song writing and as he was looking through a trade journal he saw an advert for a songwriter. He applied and at the interview the lyrics he was given were by Bernie Taupin. Elton John in a TV interview called this an amazing event and said it was 'kismet'. In becoming aware of his inner drive to move on and noting his unhappiness, Elton John opened up to individuation and embraced the resulting synchronistic occurrences, thereby sealing his destiny.

Stage Three – Life changing wake-up calls

We are unable to ignore the significant indicators of stage three as they are major and life changing events such as: job losses/businesses changing (many people are made redundant during this time); illness or disease strikes; a relationship ends (divorce, separation); a death occurs in the family or close friends. These situations have a common thread – they all require immediate attention. We cannot ignore them – we sense we are not in control of our lives any longer, we are being forced to listen and to wake up and to take action. The majority of us do take action at this stage – we re-evaluate our life - it is never too late and sometimes this stage has the most far reaching effects on the growth of the individual.

When natural and major disasters occur it often makes people re-evaluate their lives and in some cases, it acts as the wake up call and propels them into moving through individuation. For example when the Tsunami struck in 2004, the Czech model Petra Nemcova was with her boyfriend Simon Atlee in Thailand.

He died and she survived. She decided to set up the Happy Hearts Fund, a charity which operates in 11 countries and builds sustainable schools which the local community take over and manage. She also aims to implement her own scheme of connecting children via cyberspace to teach them that no matter where they are from they are all the same. The lessons she has learned from the Tsunami is that 'we are all the same, all connected and there is so little time'. Petra was only 25 when this occurred yet, she decided to take the lessons on board and grow and develop and move forward.

By taking the time to complete the questionnaire on 'Where are you on the path of Individuation' it will help you to review your life - what is occurring around you? How do you feel about the situation you are in right now? Who is important to you? Do you have an inner lack of fulfilment? This will give you clues as to where you are on your path and what you need to pay attention too at this moment. It is an intuitive and insightful exercise to awaken dormant thoughts and to help embrace change.

We need to be brave to move through the stages of individuation – but when we do, the rewards are truly great.

Questionnaire:
Where are you on the path of Individuation?

1. Do you have an inner lack of fulfilment? Yet on the surface everything appears to be perfect?

2. Can you describe this inner lack of fulfilment? – how do you feel?

3. Explain what your situation is- how old are you/ what is happening around you? Have you experience significant major changes in the last few years of your life?

4. Are you really being authentic in your interests, passions and talents ? If not, why not and what are they? ~Do you remember from childhood what held your attention?

5. Are you afraid of seeming disloyal by being more honest? If so, how and to whom ? e.g. peer pressure? work?

6. What is missing from your life?

7. What *exactly* is it about this stage of your life that is making you feel uncomfortable?

8. What is calling you? What is urging you to forge into the unknown? Have you felt this way before and if so when and how

9. What is over for you?

10. What are you still passionate about?

11. How would you like to be at this moment?

Chapter Three

What happens when we suppress individuation and why do we do this?

This chapter details the cost to ourselves (and those around us) of suppressing individuation rather than embracing it.

It shows us how it can affect every area of our lives – career, work, relationships, finances, aspirations and most significantly our health.

One of the most important area of our lives is our career, the work we do, yet so many of us allow others to dictate our career direction or path, our promotions, even to influence the company we work for. How many of us are in careers because it is our passion? Or is it because our parents, our peers or friends have influenced our choice? – because it is deemed a safe choice, it gives us a secure future....

How many of us have failed to listen to our hearts and to our passions and made a decision to pursue a career which is in conflict to our passion? When David Attenborough was working very successfully at the BBC, he was offered the position of Director General – a prestigious post. However David was unsure what to do and telephoned his brother Dickie and asked his advice. His brother said 'What do you love to do? And David told him he wanted to make documentaries about life on earth. And Dickie told him that was what he must do. He must follow his heart, his passion'. And of course he did.

Are you doing the work that you love, are passionate about – if not, do you know what it would be? Billy Mawhinney, from Northern Ireland and Creative Director at the Leo Burnett Advertising Agency was known in his town as the 'poster boy' from a very young age. He loved to draw and in particular to make posters of particular events – and although he initially did not work with his passion he then qualified in Art Design and started a very successful career in the Advertising world.

What made you ignore your passion? By not following your passion, how is it affecting your life?

When we begin to individuate we question our work – it is of course difficult to change as many factors are involved such as: financial; peer pressure; confidence and many more. It takes courage to move to a different field, retrain or take a career break. When we are in the wrong career or in a job we are not passionate about it has a detrimental spiral effect on our relationships and our health. How?

In many instances if we are in the wrong career we will have already received many wake up calls to encourage us to move - and of course if they are ignored then career success usually passes us by, our career becomes more difficult and we may lose our jobs. Once again life becomes uncomfortable.

Sadly the main cost of not individuation is that our identity is destroyed. Once this occurs we are not able to live authentically (when we individuate we automatically live authentically) and intriguingly it sets in motion numerous events that crystallize our life. For example we meet the wrong people, the opportunities we need to move to the next stage of our lives do not appear, events become obstacles not synchronistic occurrences. Regrettably life becomes difficult and relationships and health are ultimately destroyed.

Our health and well being are affected adversely when we do not individuate. We become unhappy, depressed or envious of others. We suffer from fears and anxieties. We become directionless. Ultimately, by staying in the comfort zone, we destroy our sense of identity and therefore we do not become complete or achieve our purpose or become who we destined to become. We do not fulfil our destiny. When this occurs we feel a sense of incompleteness of emptiness which increases the more we suppress our individuation.

Here, we question whether society really values the process of individuation. Sadly, it often does not or certainly not as much as we would hope.

For example, when we commit to individuation, the first thing that happens is that we have to confront our unconscious attachment to cultural myths, such as 'You are too old to change'. This is especially common when we want to pursue another career. In fact when I made the decision to leave the hotel industry at the relatively young age of 39 I was told that I would not be able to achieve another successful career and I was throwing away such a wonderful opportunity. I know that my identity was caught up in the glamorous life of the hotel industry. Similarly a very good friend Roz Savage, now an ocean rower, author and inspirational speaker, gave up her job in investment banking after questioning her life - another promotion, another dinner party in Kew - and becoming increasingly bored and restless. She knew she could not ignore the signals and now is encompassing her love of the environment in the work that she does.

And other cultural myths such as 'why can't you be satisfied with everything you have,' and 'don't rock the boat' are exceptionally common and unfortunately they allow those who are individuating to question whether they are being selfish and or should they pursue this new path. In essence, they influence their decision.

Carol Adrienne, author of 'Find your Purpose, Change your life', claims that 'cultural wisdom doesn't really value our inner drive as being all that significant and subsequently this lack of support prevents many of us from individuating fully'.

For me I realise now, it was the need to continue individuating that was the impetus for me to leave the comfort of my 'good' job and set out for the unknown. Not an easy decision and one that took a long time to make, but the rewards were very great and truly worthwhile.

To continue to grow and develop and to become more of who we are we must embrace individuation, not suppress it.

Chapter Four

The Seven Year Cycle
and Synchronistic Occurrences

Individuation is one of the major psychological life forces that attracts change into our lives, and every seven years the universe helps us to recognise its presence and assists us to embrace the changes by placing synchronistic occurrences on our path.

This chapter focuses on the synchronistic events which occur in relation to the seven year cycle. It emphasises how, when we raise our awareness of individuation we can anticipate the changes the seven year cycle may bring and be ready to act upon the synchronistic occurrences which automatically appear, as if from the universe. These are placed along our path to make our journey effortless and most importantly to encourage us to live in alignment with the universe.

However, we do not always recognise these subtle clues or if we do, we may not want to utilise these opportunities when they arise. The seven year cycle in relation to age i.e. 21, 28, 35, 42, 49, 56, 63, 70 etc as per the attached diagram is of great significance. From birth through childhood and adolescence (7, 14, to the age of 21yrs) the 7yr cycle is developmental in a physical sense – it can be seen and from 21yrs the development cycle is more mental and emotional and obviously as there is no further physical development, it is less visible, yet it is possibly even more powerful. If we use the cycle to our advantage we can prepare for change and initiate the move to the next stage of our personal growth. If we begin to plan our lives in alignment with the 7yr cycle of age then we are less likely to stagnate, less likely to be shocked by events that supposedly take us by surprise. It becomes a natural process, to embrace individuation and more a way of life.

Interestingly, it is most common for people to settle down at the age of 28yrs approximately and become more adult; 35yrs is peak career time, a time to make big commitments and changes to lifestyle; and 42/49 is when we review all aspects of our lives – possibly get divorced, enter into new relationships, develop second careers, make major changes in our lives or major changes happen to us. Madonna, got married for the second time at the age of 42yrs and got divorced seven years later at the age of 49. The ages of 56/63yrs is a time for continued achievements but possibly in a different way such as; contributing back to the community, to life and really honing our learnings and skills and passing on our knowledge and leaving a legacy. Depending on our age, if we review the diagram attached we may be able to pinpoint significant events in our lives, trigger some memories and it may allow us to recall the incidences leading up to the seven year mark – what was happening around us, who did we meet, who influenced us.

So why is seven known as the mystical number? (other numbers such as 11, 12 and 22 are also known to have great significance) however seven is mentioned throughout history. Some examples of the number seven: Seven days of the week; seven musical notes; seven archangels; seven ancient planets; seven chakras - specific energy centres known as chakras relate to a specific organ and emotional state; the moon has a cycle of 28 days, four quarterly cycles; seven is the neutral point in the ph scale. Dr. Christianne Northrup in her book 'Womens Bodies, Womens Wisdom' claims that 'our cells keep replacing themselves daily and we create a whole new body every seven years'. This very much relates to the development cycle of the human body.

Within the Masonic, seven is used frequently: seven liberal arts and sciences; King Solomon took seven yrs to build the Temple and it was dedicated to the glory of God in the seventh month; Seven brethren are needed to make a lodge. In Scriptural history there is frequent reference to the number seven; for example in Revelation 1:16 ' and he had in his right hand seven stars' alluding to the seven churches of Asia; And 'in my house there are seven mansions; Rome was built on seven hills.

In mathematical terms it is used very effectively. It is thought by early scientists that the universe is made up of numbers and sounds – it is an exact science. A profound example is the mystical number *1.618* (when added together equals seven). It is a ratio and is known by many terms such as the golden ratio 1: 1.168, or as PHI, or the divine proportion. It has mathematical origins as it is derived from the Fibonacci sequence and denotes harmony, balance and perfection. Scientists have recognised that it is the key to natural form and growth. Artists have used it to bring harmony to their compositions and Leonardo da Vinci used it extensively (i.e. in the Mona Lisa) and in his famous drawing of the human body, he used it to raise our consciousness, and our awareness of this ratio.

It is used in classical architecture to give total symmetry. It is found in the human body and in all aspects of nature – the building blocks of plants i.e. the rose is just one perfect example- and the most familiar example is the nautilus – the spiral seashell. Each of the spiral's diameters has the ratio 1.618 in relation to the next spiral. When we find things look beautiful whether in a building, animal, plant or human they will always have this number 1.618 (the ratio of 1:1.618); the divine proportion; the golden ratio; PHI – it is perfection -created by the universe? Pythagoras promoted this ratio to mean 'unity with the universe'.

As the universe nudges us to reach out, to forge into the unknown, it places synchronistic opportunities on our path to ease our way forward. Opportunities can take the form of meeting the right person at the right time, being in the right place at the right time and or developing specific and influential partnerships with another.

Further examples of other fascinating partnerships, similar to Elton John and Bernie Taupin, who were mentioned in an earlier chapter, which have occurred at just the right time i.e. synchronistically, are detailed here. One of the most inspiring and significant partnerships, even magical is that of Audrey Hepburn and Hubert de Givenchy. Seemingly, from an excerpt from the book 'How to be lovely' by Melissa Hellstern, Givenchy was told that a Miss Hepburn was coming to look at some clothes and he immediately thought of Katharine. Audrey was looking for clothes for her new movie, 'Sabrina'. Her latest film, 'Roman Holiday ' had not yet been released in Europe therefore she was relatively unknown. However, even though Givenchy was in the middle of a collection and could not make her any clothes she tried on those already made and they were perfect. The clothes she chose for this film became an immediate success and were known as *décolleté Sabrina*. He took her out to dinner and he said 'it was then she truly won my heart'. This was the start of their lifelong collaboration – and the beginning of a deep friendship.

Another influential designer, Valentino met his future finance director and future partner when he was waiting in a queue to enter a club. He saw an empty seat on a table and he asked if he could sit to wait and that was it – this was the beginning of their lifelong partnership in business. In history, there have been many wonderful partnerships, some it is frequently said are 'made in heaven' as they complement each other so perfectly, such as: Queen Victoria and Albert who became a moving and formidable partnership – he died when only 42yrs old. Queen Elizabeth 11, has a memorable and wonderful marriage and partnership with Prince Philip whom she met when she was just 13yrs old.

Richard and Judy, ex TV presenters show us a wonderful example of the significance of the seven year cycle in relation to major events and to partnerships. They met once again quite synchronistically at GMTV where she was his mentor or known as 'mummy'. They were with GMTV for a total of 14yrs. Before leaving GMTV, for Channel 4 their final two years had been fraught with differences of opinions with new producers and they had became uncomfortable with an inner sense of dissatis-faction - significant indicators to move on. Again, the first stages of individuation. Interestingly, they left channel four after seven years and again the final two years were difficult, having to share the slot with another presenter.

Meeting influential people/partners is significant of course, a significant opportunity however, synchronistic events appear even more frequently to help guide us in the right direction. When we became more aware we can easily recognise these occurrences and use them proactively. For example when Prince Charles was in his early twenties and first heard of the Brixton riots which were very serious, of huge media interest and continued for a long time, he asked the question 'What can I do to help', to make a difference to these young peoples lives?' – it was then that the Princes Trust came into being. This was the trigger, the event. He also has said his great interest in archi-tecture and traditional and classical buildings was the result of spending his early childhood in the grand surroundings of Buckingham Palace- was this one of the things he was being prepared for as a prince? As the Prince of Wales he has been given time to implement all his innovative and futuristic ideas before he takes the throne. Wisely he has utilised this time and he has now become widely admired and a respected successor to the throne.

When Christopher Bailey, Creative Director of luxury brand Burberry, decided to leave Gucci, a job he absolutely loved, but knew it was the right time to move on, he decided to take time out and wait. He also had a trigger, an event – his grandmother was seriously ill – in taking time out and having time to think and after a period of time, he was then offered his new position at Burberry – a perfect next step. We need to always be aware of the signs and have the courage to know when it is right to move. Also we need to know that there is always a waiting time when we go through the process of individuation – it is never immediate. Individuation is our ally, here to assist us and guide us – to achieve our destiny.

Elton John has used the word 'kismet' and Rod Stewart the word fate when describing pivotal or amazing happenings in their career. We all are amazed when things happen as if by magic and everything falls into place. When Rod Stewart asked for a train set one birthday his father gave him a guitar instead, that is a significant event.

Similarly Steven Spielberg was given a video recorder by his parents on his 14th birthday – again an event. We may all have experienced events such as this. When Rod Steward was in the group The Faces, and starting to develop a solo career he recorded a single called Maggie May – it was the one that would make him famous. However it was on the 'b' side of the record not the 'a' side. A DJ in Cleveland flipped it over to the 'b' side one night and just played it. It became an instant hit and Rod described this event as a 'twist of fate'. He has said during an interview that 'God made a Rock Star' – he put him on this earth to sing'. In reality these moments or events or twists of fate are there to propel us, very fast, to what we must do next, in alignment with the universe.

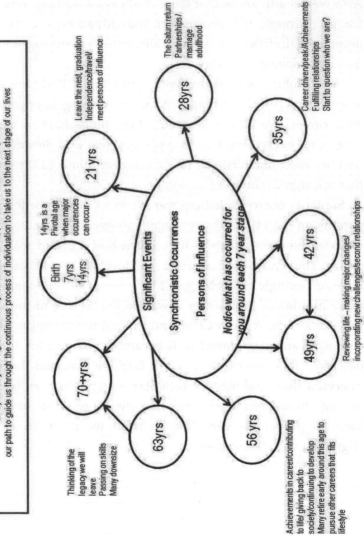

The Seven Year Cycle of Development

Every seven years significant and synchronistic events, persons of influence are put on our path to guide us through the continuous process of individuation to take us to the next stage of our lives

Significant Events

Synchronistic Occurrences

Persons of Influence

Notice what has occurred for you around each 7 year stage

Birth
7yrs
14yrs

14yrs is a Pivotal age when major occurences can occur -

21 yrs

Leave the nest, graduation Independence/travel/ meet persons of influence

28yrs

The Saturn return Partnerships/ marriage adulthood

35yrs

Career driven/peak/Achievements Fulfilling relationships Start to question who we are?

42 yrs

49yrs

Reviewing life – making major changes/ incorporating new challenges/second relationships

56 yrs

Achievements in career/contributing to life/ giving back to society/continuing to develop Many retire early around this age to pursue other careers that fits lifestyle

63yrs

70+yrs

Thinking of the legacy we will leave Passing on skills Many downsize

Johann Wolfgang von Goethe
Until one is committed, there is always the chance to draw back; always ineffectiveness
Concerning all acts of initiative (and creation) there is one elementary truth, the ignorance of which kills countless ideas and splendid plans:
That the moment one definitely commits oneself,
Then Providence moves too
All sorts of things occur to help one that would not otherwise have occurred. A whole stream of events issues from the decision, raising in one's favour all manner of unforeseen incidents and meetings and material assistance which no man could have dreamed would come his way.
Whatever you can do, or dream you can, begin it! Boldness has genius, magic and power in it
Begin it now!

Chapter Five

What are you being prepared for in life? What is your reason for being?

This is possibly one of the most important and interesting aspects to acknowledge when moving through individuation. Paulo Coelho, author, writes in 'The Alchemist', one of his most famous books *'that people learn early in their lives what is their reason for being and maybe that is why they give up on it so early too'*.

To recognise what you have been prepared for in life, it is necessary to look back at your youth; early teens, and or early family life. In conjunction with this it is essential to acknowledge those persons who were influential in your life at this early stage, not only your parents but especially those on the peripheral. Our circumstances family and early life are of particular importance and relevance to our future as they give us subtle clues as to what we may become and what our destinies could be. It is in our youth that we are first prepared for what we are to do in this world and then later again in our twenties or older that we are prepared adequately to make our own unique contributions to mankind in accordance with our destiny. It is up to us though to recognise the teachings and guidance and to take action. As you individuate, this knowledge makes the process easier and also guides you to understand 'what is your reason for being' and to move towards what you need to do to contribute effectively to your life.

This chapter gives wonderful examples of those in the public eye who have discovered their reason for being and have utilised the experience effectively. For example, Bill Clinton. He had a difficult childhood and grew up in small town America with an abusive stepfather. His family portrayed themselves as the all

American family, yet they were the antithesis of this. They were living parallel lives. Clinton claimed that he was being prepared for the job of being President in early life as it entailed being able to lead 'parallel lives'. This gave him the knowledge to enable him to become one of the most charismatic and some would say successful Presidents in history.

Madonna, the most successful female artist of all times has said that her father's discipline and strictness throughout her early life, and her mother's early death has made her who she is today. She says 'that his strictness taught her a certain amount of discipline that has ' helped me in my life and my career and also made me work harder for things...' Her mother died when she was very young and this again has affected her reason for being. 'In that period when I was losing her has a lot to do with my fuel so to speak, my fuel for life. It left me with an intense longing to fill a sort of emptiness'.

Think back to your early childhood and youth what significant events occurred? Who influenced you? What situations were you placed in? In many cases the situations were difficult, adverse not always pleasant – Norman Vincent Peale, the god father of positive thinking and the author of many books including 'The power of Positive Thinking', was brought up in a family were public speaking was the norm. He detested it, yet, had to perform regularly and in time became a preacher and an inspirational speaker who gave lectures worldwide.

A friend and colleague, David Lewis, a fulltime illustrator, caricaturist and cartoonist remembers drawing recognisable caricatures of relatives from the age of 5 probably inspired by Tintin books and encouraged by the reaction of the people he'd drawn. He honed his skills drawing teachers and the teachers he drew the most were those whose lessons least inspired him. Again situations became part of his preparation. When did he realise he could make a living from this? – when he was asked to hand over his best caricatures to be auctioned for charity. An opportunity comes along or a synchronistic event to guide you to the next stage – it is up to us whether we take it or not....

When and how did your skills become recognised? Maybe they were not so pronounced as in the above examples - what did you enjoy doing naturally? Did a situation appear in your life to enable you to utilise gifts that may have been hidden?

The sculptor, Willard Wigan was branded stupid and insignificant at school and is now collected by the Obamas, Philip Green and Simon Cowell. He makes the smallest artworks in the world. At school he started to work on a scale too small to criticise and as he walked with his head bowed he began to notice the minute things and life in the ground all around him – he started to create small things when he was about five as his parents were poor and could not afford toys. His biggest fan was his mother who always said to him 'take it smaller Willard'. In this example Willard had to endure great hardship at school and at home to awaken his talent. Although he found school and his teachers exceptionally painful, it was in this arena that his talent was brought forth – this is what he was being prepared for- and blossomed – through adversity. In a way, awakening 'talent' especially 'great talent' has to be worked for.

The Russian model, Natalia Vodianova grew up in relative poverty, in a bleak industrial town just outside Moscow, with her mother and grandparents and a disabled sister. Looking after her sister during the day she had nowhere to take her to play, that was secure and fun. When she became a successful model and entrepreneur she started the Naked Heart Foundation which builds playgrounds for inner-city children, with disabled areas, across Russia. Her first playground was built in her home town – a payback for all the years she spent with her sister without a place to play or to go to. She is giving back and contributing effectively to life – her aim is to have 500 or more such playgrounds. This is one of her reasons for being.

What is your reason for being? What are or/were you being

prepared for. How can you contribute effectively to life?

Finally a wonderful example of ' a reason for being', 'what you are being prepared for' which takes in all the influences, nudges and synchronistic occurrences that assist us to ascertain our reason for being is that of Patrick Moore, the world famous astronomer. His Story:

He was unable to attend school due to a heart condition and when he was six years old his mother gave him a book, Story of the Solar System by GF Chambers. This book awakened a deep passion within him. Near his home lived Alan Hanbury, a multimillionaire who had a small observatory in his garden. This was managed by an astronomer called WS Franks who taught Patrick how to run it. When Patrick was 14years old, Franks was killed in a car accident and Hanbury asked him to take over the running of the observatory.

This is a superb example of the evidence of:

a. situation – Patrick was ill and could not go to school; he lived near Alan Hanbury who had an observatory in his garden

b. persons of influence – his mother, giving him a book that would awaken his passion at such a young age – 6 (almost 7). Alan Hanbury, WS Franks.

c. significant events – Franks who taught Patrick how to run the observatory. Hanbury who asked him to take over the running of it

d. synchronistic occurrences – They lived near Alan Hanbury who had an observatory. WS Franks was killed

e. Age: two significant ages – 6/7 and 14yrs old.

Chapter Six

On The Path to Individuation
– The Steps

Using the questionnaire answers from chapter three ' Where are you on the Path of Individuation' which helps clarify the stage you are at and how individuation is making its presence known in your life, you can now incorporate this information into the attached diagram which outlines the steps needed to help you individuate fully by:

a. Re-evaluating your life to date – what has true value? How do I do this: Look at all aspects of your life – e.g. your work, relationships, health, finances, friendships, and decide what you truly value and the reasons why. What changes do you need to make – do you need to take time out? What is missing from your life? Once you ascertain what is missing it helps you initiate change and allows what you need to come into your life.

b. Reviewing how individuation is making its presence known, what are the significant indicators? What stage are you at – is it the first stage or the second - the whispers or the third – the loud wake up calls. What age are you? Individuation is a continuous process appearing every seven years to nudge you to the next stage. Where are you on it – for example if you are 42, a pivotal age for individuating as it usually has the most dramatic changes at this time – look back to the age of 35 – what happened then – did you suppress individuating at that time or did you move through it –how did you feel, what did you learn?

c. Reviewing the life cycle so far – the story so far i.e. what were you being prepared for; the seven year cycle; influential people; and significant events, review your questionnaires and build up the picture.

d. Re-discovering your passion – again the earlier exercise will have triggered your thoughts on what you are passionate about. Knowing what you are passionate about is a fundamental principle of success.

e. Understanding the seven groups of qualities: ENERGY; MASTERY; ONE-POINTEDNESS; DETERMINATION; PERSISTENCE; COURAGE; ORGANISATION - expressing the seven qualities when you take action throughout the process of individuation, develops your focus and makes your journey harmonious; purposeful and effortless.

Note: Seven qualities by Roberto Assagioli from the book 'What We May Be' by Piero Ferrucci

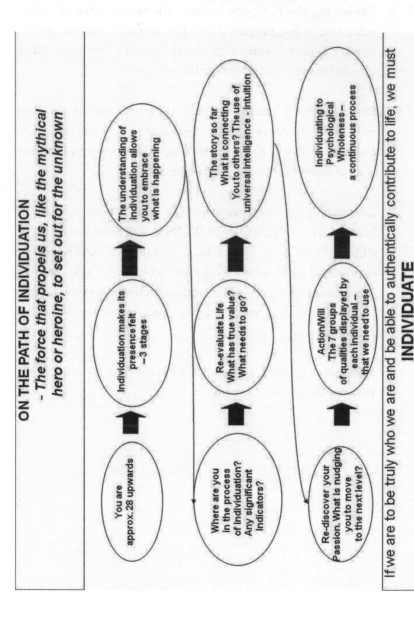

ON THE PATH OF INDIVIDUATION
- The force that propels us, like the mythical hero or heroine, to set out for the unknown

You are approx. 28 upwards

Individuation makes its presence felt – 3 stages

The understanding of Individuation allows you to embrace what is happening

Where are you in the process of Individuation? Any significant Indicators?

Re-evaluate Life What has true value? What needs to go?

The story so far What is connecting You to others? The use of universal intelligence - Intuition

Re-discover your Passion. What is nudging you to move to the next level?

Action/Will The 7 groups of qualities displayed by each individual – that we need to use

Individuating to Psychological Wholeness – a continuous process

If we are to be truly who we are and be able to authentically contribute to life, we must **INDIVIDUATE**

Chapter Seven

The Life Cycle of Individuation

This chapter gives an understanding of the life cycle of individuation – it is a continuous process, each stage or step like climbing a ladder, moving us closer to our destiny and achieving our ultimate purpose, similar to the tree of life in the Kabbalah. Every seven years, as we are continuing to individuate, we move up another step on the ladder – we learn more, we become more fulfilled and we meet new challenges to assist our soul in growing.

It gives the example, via diagram, of Audrey Hepburn's successful cycle of individuation. Starting with her early life in Austria during the war, where a severe shortage of food gave her an eating disorder in later life, it shows clearly the process of her individuation through significant events, influential people/ partnerships, major events, and the seven year cycle emphasising synchronistic occurrences. It ends with her death at the age of 63years - her 9th seven year cycle.

Towards the end of her life, her fame and status in the world gave her the opportunity to work with UNICEF as an ambassador. Her contribution was to help highlight the plight of starving children – something *she had been prepared for*. She had been given the experience in early childhood during the war with widespread food shortages. In a sense her life had come full circle.

Elton John was mentioned towards the beginning of this book and I feel he is an important example of someone who is continuing to individuate successfully. He is effectively contributing to life, i.e. giving back through the Aids Foundation he set up many years ago. Again through his own homosexuality and coming to terms with it, he has been prepared for this and utilised his learnings to help others – the essence of contributing to life. He is acknowledging along with his music his humanitarian purpose in life.

During the continuous process of individuation and the changes we make on average every seven years in line with this process we can contribute to life or give back and use our experiences of what we have been prepared for at any stage – sometimes we are able to do this at a relatively young age. For example although mentioned in an earlier chapter the model Natalia Vodianova, and previously one of the faces for Calvin Klein is only in her late twenties but has already taken the opportunity to contribute back to life, to give back – through her Naked Heart Foundation. Calvin Klein is quoted in Harpers Bazaar magazine as saying 'Natalia is an inspiration to me, she was not handed her success; she comes from a very modest background which contributed to her desire to give back. She has quietly and resolutely gone about touching people's lives in a positive way'.

We can give back whenever the opportunity arises, in any way that we wish, large or small, however it seems the more you give back and the earlier we do it the more we receive in return. Madonna and Oprah both only in their early fifties have continuously given back from the start of their fame.

Review your own individuation cycle

The blank individuation diagram gives you, the reader, the opportunity to review your own individuation cycle. By using the cycle diagram as a guideline, and utilising the information from the questionnaires and exercises in previous chapters you can pin point all the significant indicators which have occurred along your path so far. It also highlights what we are being prepared for next, to continue to successfully individuate and to achieve our destiny and live a life with purpose.

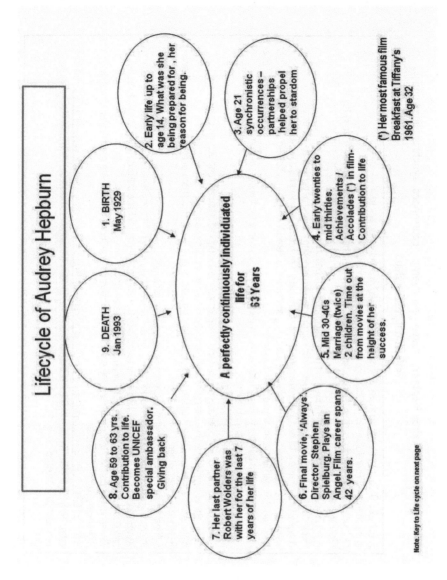

Lifecycle of Audrey Hepburn

1. BIRTH May 1929

9. DEATH Jan 1993

2. Early life up to age 14. What was she being prepared for, her reason for being.

3. Age 21 synchronistic occurrences — partnerships helped propel her to stardom

A perfectly continuously individuated life for 63 Years

4. Early twenties to mid thirties. Achievements / Accolades (*) in film - Contribution to life

5. Mid 30-40s Marriage (twice) 2 children. Time out from movies at the height of her success.

6. Final movie, 'Always'. Director Stephen Spielburg. Plays an Angel. Film career spans 42 years.

7. Her last partner Robert Wolders was with her for the last 7 years of her life

8. Age 59 to 63 yrs. Contribution to life. Becomes UNICEF special ambassador. Giving back

(*) Her most famous film Breakfast at Tiffany's 1961. Age 32

Note. Key to Life cycle on next page

Key - Lifecycle of Audrey Hepburn; seven year events, occurrences, synchronicities and influential partnerships

2. Early life 0- 21yrs: Lived through war. Shortage of food gave her slight eating disorder and became very careful with her diet. Dancing became a distraction through the war. Mother had victorian values - provided discipline and pushed her to great heights. Father had left the family home. Close to grandparents.

Age 12 – dance led her to Amsterdam after the war taken back to London to Ballet Rambert school. Wanted to be a ballet dancer however needed to earn money did modelling and had bit parts as an actress.

3. Age 21yrs: offered a 'bit part' in a movie called Monte Carlo baby. The French playwright Sidonie-Gabrielle Collete was staying in the same hotel where they were shooting and instantly offered Audrey the part of Gigi, on Broadway in New York. Her dancing talent helped clinch the role.

At the same time the Director William Wyler saw her screen test and cast her as the Princess in Roman Holiday – he had been looking for an unknown.

Met Hubert de Givenchy – destined to meet – and collaborated with her all on her films.

4. Age 28/early thirties: – Accolades, achievements, awards became a sought after film star and fashion icon.

At the age of 32yrs made Breakfast at Tiffany's which became her most famous film.

5. Mid 30s – 40s married twice had two children and took time out to be at home. Used her creative abilities in art – painting. Relished being a mother.

6. Final movie – 'Always' directed by Steven Spielberg. Plays an angel.

Interesting fact as taken from the book Audreystyle, by Pamela Clarke Keogh:' When Steven Spielberg was a teenager living in Arizona, he was taken kicking and screaming by his parents to see funny Face at the drive in. The moment he saw Audrey he was mesmerized and he fell in love with her and film.

7. Met her last partner Robert Wolder at the age of 56 (had grown up together just a few miles apart but had never met). She said he was her soul mate.

8. Age 59-63 UNICEF special ambassador – she was giving something back and this is what she was being prepared for in her early life and her life as a movie star then prepared her for the next stage – to be on the international stage as an ambassador and not a movie star.

The Life Cycle of Individuation

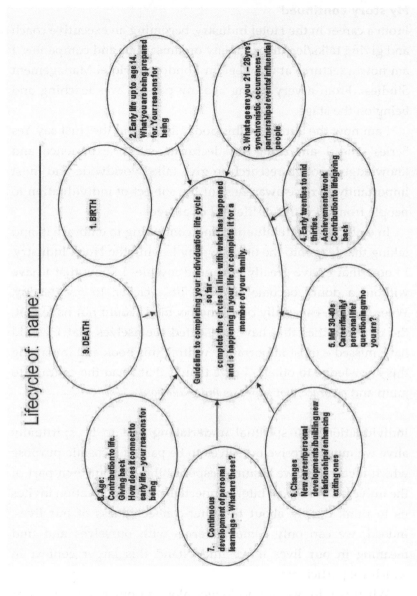

Lifecycle of name:

1. BIRTH

2. Early life up to age 14.
What you are being prepared for. Your reasons for being

3. What age are you 21 – 28yrs? synchronistic occurrences – partnerships/ events/ influential people

9. DEATH

Guideline to completing your individuation life cycle so far –
complete the circles in line with what has happened and is happening in your life or complete it for a member of your family.

4. Early twenties to mid thirties.
Achievements/work
Contribution to life/giving back

8. Age:
Contribution to life.
Giving back
How does it connect to early life – your reasons for being

7. Continuous development of personal learnings – What are these?

6. Changes
New career/personal developments /building new relationships/ enhancing exiting ones

5. Mid 30–40s
Career/family/ personal life/ questioning who you are?

41

My story continued

From a career in the Hotel Industry, becoming an executive coach and giving talks/lectures to many organisations and companies, I am now a lecturer at a college in London in Hotel Management Studies.. From a very young age my passion was teaching and being on the stage.

I am now the author of this book, the first in the 'Just say Yes Series' and I am using my lecturing skills, experience and knowledge through research to give talks worldwide and most importantly to raise awareness of the subject of individuation to people from all walks of life and of all ages.

In embracing individuation and continuing to embrace it, and taking that leap into the unknown by leaving the Hotel Industry, I know that I have greatly enhanced my life. I know that I have without a doubt become closer, a little closer, to my destiny. When I think, especially of all the people I would not have met, the opportunities that have presented themselves that I would have missed – most importantly writing this book and imparting this knowledge to others- I give thanks that I had the courage to jump and *embrace, not suppress individuation!*

Individuation is a spiritual undertaking and to be spiritually alive we must perceive ourselves to be part of a cosmic purpose which means that we assume responsibility for our own part of the universe. We are all inter-connected and individuation invites us to think deeply about the inter-connectedness of our lives. Indeed, we can only come to terms with ourselves and find meaning in our lives if we understand this larger context in which we participate.

When we do, we are no longer alone in our psyche and our whole world view is altered. Then individuation becomes a way of life and gives meaning to life and gives us the understanding that, to fulfil our human potential, we must individuate.

Our lives are so much richer than we allow them to be and

what we need to do is to collaborate with the world, the universe,
by taking action and to:

Just say Yes to Individuation!

Bibliography

Adrienne Carol: The Purpose of your Life; Find your Purpose and Change your Life, Harpercollins, 2001

Anodea Judith: Wheels of Life, Llewellyn Publications, 1987

Coelho Paulo: The Alchemist, Thorsons, 1998

Ferrucci Piero: What we may be, Penguin/Putnam, 1982

Hamilton David: It's the Thought that Counts, Hay House, 2005

Hellstern, Melissa: How to be lovely, Penguin, 2004

Hollis James: The Middle Passage, Inner City Books, 1993

Hopkin C. J. M.: The Practical Kabbalah Guidebook, Godsfield Press, 2001

Jaworski Joseph: Synchronicity: The Inner Path of Leadership, Berrett-Koehler Publishers, 2006

Myss Caroline: Anatomy of the Spirit, Bantam Books, 1997

Northrup Christiane Dr: Women's Bodies, Women's Wisdom, Piatkus, 1995

Quindlen Anna: A Short Guide to a Happy Life, Century, 2002

Readers Digest: Exploring the Unkown, Readers Digest Association, 1999

St Michael Mick: 'Madonna Talking', Omnibus Press, 2004

Schultz, Mona Lisa: Awakening Intuition, Harmony Books, 1998

Scovel-Shinn Florence: The Game of Life and How to Play it, Vermilion (imprint of Ebury Publishing), 2005

Storr Anthony: The Essential Jung, Fontana Press, 1998

BOOKS

MySpIRITRaDIo